B. Harris Cowper

The Journal of Sacred Literature and Biblical Record

B. Harris Cowper

The Journal of Sacred Literature and Biblical Record

ISBN/EAN: 9783337243821

Printed in Europe, USA, Canada, Australia, Japan

Cover: Foto ©Lupo / pixelio.de

More available books at **www.hansebooks.com**

THE

JOURNAL

OF

SACRED LITERATURE

AND

BIBLICAL RECORD.

EDITED BY

B. HARRIS COWPER,

EDITOR OF THE NEW TESTAMENT IN GREEK FROM CODEX A; A SYRIAC GRAMMAR, ETC.

VOL. VII. (New Series.)

WILLIAMS AND NORGATE,

14 HENRIETTA STREET, COVENT GARDEN, LONDON;

20 SOUTH FREDERICK STREET, EDINBURGH.

1865.

.[P]

° B. .

[P] B. .

 (cf. 15.)
h B. adds o.   i B.
k B. .   l B. .
m B. .   n B. .

⁖   ⁖   ⁖   ⁖   ⁖

.

 [b]
، (fol. 44)
 [c]
 [d]
---

w B. .   **x** B. .   **y** B. ||.

z B. .   **a** B. adds |.   **b** B. .

c Altered by a later hand into .   **d** B. |||.

e B. ||.

 B. ‏ B. ‏ B. ‏.

 B. ‏ B. ‏ B. ‏.

(fol. 43)
 P
---

1 B. .   m B. .   n B. omits .

o B. .   B. .

ܩܕܝܫ ܩܕܝܫ.° ܘܟܕ ܡܪܢ ܝܫܘܥ (fol. 42) ܐܬܬܐ ܕܝܢ ܡܪܬܝ،
ܡܪܝܡ. ܦܢܬ ܠܗ̇ ܘܐܡܪܬ ܡܪܝܡ. ܗܘܝܬ. ܘܡܫܒܚܐ
ܐܬܢܫܩܬ ܘܣܓܕܬ ܠܗ. ܘܐܡܪ ܠܗ̇ ܡܪܢ ܝܫܘܥ.
ܐܚܘܬܐ ܠܟ ܫܘܒܚܐ ܕܥܠܬ ܐܢܬ ܐܬܐܡܪ. ܐܡܪܐ
ܠܗ ܠܬܠܡܝܕܐ ܡܪܝܡ. ܠܟܐܢܬ ܙܟܘܬ. ܘܐܬܦܬ ܝܫܘ
ܡܪܢ ܘܝܫܘ ܡܪܬܝ، ܡܪܝܡ ܐܠܗܐ ܢܒܝܐ. ܘܫܘܒܚ
ܘܬܫܒܘܚܬܐ ܘܫܘܒܚܐ ܒܐܦܝܐ. ܗܠܝܢ ܐܬܘ ܒܪܡܫܐ ܕܪܘܡ
ܠܦܪܕܝܣܐ ܕܥܕܢ. ܘܐܡܪ ܠܗ̇ ܡܪܢ ܠܐܡܗ. ܡܪܝܡ
ܐܬܦܢܝ ܘܚܙܝ، ܡܕܡ ܕܡܬܦܢܝܢ ܠ ܠܦܪܕܝܣܐ ܕܐܚܝܕܢ. ܚܙܝܬ
ܕܝܢ ܗ، ܠܬܫܒܘܚܬܐ ܒܢܘܗܝ ܗܠܝܢ ܕܦܪܕܝܣܐ ܕܐܡܝܢܐ ܢܨܝܒܝܢ
ܘܫܦܝܪܝܢ ܘܦܐܝܝܢ. ܘܚܙܬ ܒܗܘܢ ܩܘܡܬܐ ܕܩܘܕܫܐ.ᵈ ܘܚܙܬ
ܒܗܘ ܒܢܘܢ ܫܒܝܠܐ ܕܒܢ̈ܝܢܐ ܦܫܝܛܝܢ ܒܗ. ܘܚܙܬ
ܠܐܝܠܢܐ ܐܪ̈ܙܝܐᵉ ܕܦܪܕܝܣܐ ܕܒܗ ܫܩܝܪܝܢ ܒܩܢܘܡܗܘܢᶠ
ܘܟܘܚܒܐ ܐܦ ܢܘܗܪܐ ܕܩܘܕܫܗܘܢ. ܘܐܬܢܚ ܒܗܘܢ ܐܝܠܢܐ
ܠܐܝܠܢܐ ܗܪ̈ܘܡܐ. ܘܒܗܘܢ ܗܘ̈ܒܐ ܠܗܘ̈ܒܐ ܚܠܦ ܚܠܦܐ
ܒܗܒܒܐ. ܘܢܦܠܬ ܡܪܢ ܝܫܘܥ ܡܢ ܦܐܪ̈ܐ ܬܪ̈ܝܨܐ ܗܠܝܢ
ܕܐܝܠܢܐᵍ ܘܚܙܬ ܠܗ̇ ܕܐܬܓܠܝܢʰ ܡܢ ܗܠܝܢ ܐܝ̈ܠܢܐ ܕܐܬܪܟܒܘ
ܒܪܘܚܐ ܕܩܘܕܫܐ ❖ ❖ ❖ ܗܠܝܢ ܚܙܬ ܡܪܬܝ، ܡܪܝܡ
ܒܦܪܕܝܣܐ ܕܥܕܢ. ܘܒܬܪܟܐ ܒܪܘܟܐ ܕܫܡܝܐ ܐܚܕ ܘܫܠܠ
ܘܐܡܪ ܠܗ̇ ܡܪܢ ܠܐܡܗ. ܬܘ، ܗܫܐ ܘܚܙܝ، ܫܡܝܐ ܕܐܝܟ ܐܢܬܝ
ܒܚܓܝܗܘܢ ܕܐܝܟ. ܘܢܦܠܬ، ܘܚܙܬ، ܫܡܝ̈ܐ ܫܡܝܐ ܘܫܡ̈ܝܐ
ܕܠܥܠ ܡܢ ܫܡܝܐ. ܘܡܢ ܬܡܢ ܘܠܥܠ ܦܠܛܬⁱ ܘܪܗܛܬᵏ

ᶜ B. adds ܩܕܝܫ.   ᵈ B. adds ܩܕܝܫܐ.   ᵉ B. ܪ̈ܘܚܢܐ.
ᶠ B. ܒܩܢܘܡܗܘܢ.   ᵍ B. ܘܕܝܠܗ ܬܠܡ̈ܝܕܐ.   ʰ B. ܕܬܬܓܠܝܢ.
ⁱ B. ܦܠܛܬ.   ᵏ B. ܘܪܗܛܬ.

ˣ B.   ʸ B.   ᶻ B.

ᵃ B.   ᵇ B.

 (fol. 41)

ᵍ B. .   ᵗ B. .

ᵘ B. .

 (fol. 40)

° B. .

ᵠ B. .

ᴾ B. .

ʳ B. .

<hr>

[i] B. adds .

[l] B. , adding .

[k] B. .

[m] B. .

 (fol. 39)
c B. .   d B. .   e B. .

f B. .   g B. .   h B. .

(fol. 38)

ᵛ B. ܡܛܪ̈. ʷ B. ܠܗܘܢ. ˣ B. ܘܒܓܘܗ.

ʸ B. ܐܚܕܘ. ᶻ B. ܘܡܚܘܙܚܡ. ᵃ B. ܟܬܢܬܝܐ.

ᵇ B. ܘܡܚܘܙܚܡ.

<p>
<q>.

[Syriac text, 18 lines]

(fol. 37)

---

f B. adds [Syriac].   g B. [Syriac].   h B. [Syriac].

i B. [Syriac].   k B. omits [Syriac].

l B. adds [Syriac].   m B. [Syriac].   n B. [Syriac].

o B. [Syriac].

 [b].
✦ ✦ ✦ [c]
✧   ✧   ✧   ✧

.

[d] [e]
[w] B. adds :	[x] B. .	[y] B. .
[z] B. .	[a] B. .	[b] B. .
[c] B. adds .	[d] B. .	[e] B. .

 (fol. 36) .
 B. B. adds B. .

 B. B. B. adds

 (fol. 35) .

THE DEPARTURE OF MY LADY MARY FROM THIS WORLD.[a]

Book First.

The peace of God, who sent His Son and he came into the world : and the peace of the Son, who migrated from heaven and dwelt in Mary : and the peace of the Holy Spirit, the τραγῳδός who sings and the Paraclete who is besung : the peace of the Lord of created beings, the glory of whose Godhead created beings are not able to comprehend ; who left the chariot that is adorned in the supernal heights, and descended and dwelt in the bosom of Mary : be with us and with all our congregation, and bless[b] the crown (or garland) of the priests our fathers, who sit at the head of us all and of our flock, for ever and ever.   Amen.

Open, Lord, the gates of heaven to our prayers at this time, and let a sweet perfume ascend from our congregations to the supernal ranks ;[c] and let the trumpets of the archangels sound in heaven, and the bands of the supernals stand rank on rank ; and let there be praise in heaven before the exalted King ; and from all the mansions of the Father's house let the voices of the guardian angels (ἐγρήγοροι) sing ; and let troops stand facing troops, and ranks beside ranks, and armies opposite armies ; and let there be praise and a sweet perfume before God, and also thanksgiving and worship to the Messiah, and laudations and praises to the Holy Spirit.

The exit of my Lady Mary from this world, our brethren, we call to mind before you.   Command, Lord, a blessing and a good reward upon the ministry, that they may glorify ; and upon the rich, that they may laud ; and upon the poor, that they may become rich ; and upon the old men, that they may praise ; and upon the youths, that they may bless.   And the women, the daughters of Eve, answer them, Lord, in prayer, when they cry to Thee ; for from them was chosen the woman, the virgin and holy,[d] whom her Lord chose from all women, and

---

[a] B. "The history of Mary, the mother of God."—Since the Syriac text of this book was printed, I have been permitted, through the kindness of my friend Hofrath Dr. Tischendorf, to peruse the original Greek, which he has discovered and intends shortly to edit.   The Syriac translation has, I find, been greatly amplified in various ways, such passages as the introduction, narrating the discovery of the book, the disputation before the Hēgemōn, the liturgical portions of the fourth book, and the like, being all later additions.   The Greek text is not divided into books.

[b] B. "and let be blessed."

[c] B. "to the ranks of the supernals."   [d] B. "the holy virgin."

of her was born the Lord of glory, the Son of the living God, to whom be glory, and to her a good memorial, for ever. Blessed be Thy grace, God that didst die, King's son that wast debased, Undying that didst will and die; who didst migrate from the Father unto Mary, and from Mary to the manger, and from the manger to the circumcision, and from the circumcision to bringing up, and from bringing up to stripes, and from stripes to blows, and from blows to the Cross, and from the Cross to death, and from death to the grave, and from the grave to the resurrection, and from the resurrection to Heaven, and sittest, lo, at the right hand of Thy Father. Stretch forth, Lord, Thy right hand from the exalted throne of Thy glory at this time, and bless, Lord, our congregation, that exalts the commemoration of Thy mother, my Lady Mary, Thou Lord God.

And ye, believing hearers, hearers of the coronation of my Lady Mary, let every one that believes in the Father who is undivided, assert and confess that God sent His Son, and that He was born of Mary the Virgin, without marriage, as saith Isaiah the prophet, the most glorious of the prophets: " He grew up before him as a tender plant, and as a root out of a dry ground ;"ᵉ and again he says: " Behold, a virgin shall conceive and bear a son, and they shall call his name Immanuel,"ᶠ which is, being interpreted, our God is with us. For the blessed (Virgin) too was holy and elect of God from (the time) when she was in her mother's womb; and she was born of her mother gloriously and holily; and she purified herself from all evil thoughts, that she might receive the Messiah her Lord, who came unto her, that through His being born of her He might give life to the people who believe in Him.ᵍ Consequently,ʰ this is the woman whose memory we should celebrate; this is the blessed among women, of whom was born the Saviour of all mankind ;ⁱ this is the land of blessings, of which was born the husbandman of gladness,ʲ that by his going forth into the world he might root up the thorns, and burn the tares, and destroy error, and annihilate death, and drive away Satan, and make concord reign, and sow peace over all the regions of the world.

Now then we make mention before you concerning this book of my Lady Mary, how it was revealed at this time.

ᵉ Isa. liii. 2. ᶠ Isa. vii. 14.

ᵍ *Literally*, " to the world that believes in him ;" but ܚܠܟܐ, عَالَم, is here used in much the same sense as " tout le monde," " all the world."

ʰ This word is wanting in B.

ⁱ *Lit.* " creatures," *or* " created things." ʲ B. " of joys."

Certain men on Mount Sinai,[k] Mār David the presbyter, and Mār John the presbyter, and Mār Philip the deacon, were much concerned,—because these three holy men were at the altar which was placed on the summit of Mount Sinai, where was the thornbush, out of which the Lord spake with Moses, and were the officiating priests of the shrine[l] that was built there,—and they wrote letters and sent them to Cyrus[m] the bishop, that his holiness might take much pains. And they asked therein concerning the book of my Lady Mary, how she had departed from this world; "because we have a great desire to know with what glory she was crowned." And when the letter was written from Mount Sinai, brethren came and brought it to Jerusalem, and it was read before the whole people; and they sought for the book of my Lady Mary and did not find it; but they found a book in which was written thus: "I James, bishop of Jerusalem, have written with my own hands in this volume, that in the year 345 my Lady Mary departed from this world; and there were written concerning her six books, each book by two of the apostles; and I testify (with regard to) these books which were written, that John the young[n] used to carry them, and also Paul and Peter know where they are, because they went along with them from Jerusalem." And when Cyrus, bishop of Jerusalem, sought for the book of my Lady Mary and they did not find it, they wrote[o] a letter to Mount Sinai (as follows). "From Cyrus, bishop of Jerusalem, and the whole clergy, to our brethren the priests and our fathers who are on Mount Sinai, much peace. The letter which came to us from you, we have received; and we have made inquiries in Jerusalem concerning the book of the departure of my Lady Mary, but we have not found it. We have found, however, an autograph (note) of James written thus; 'The six books which were written about the death of my Lady Mary, John the young, whose blessedness is great, used to carry them, and Paul and Peter and John the young know where they are, because they went along with them from Jerusalem.'" And at the request of Cyrus, bishop of Jerusalem, ...[p] they assembled the

---

[k] See Enger, p. 11, "Erant in sancto monte Sinai," etc.

[l] *Lit.* "place of martyrs," place where the relics of martyrs are preserved, μαρτύριον.

[m] Apparently *Cyriacus*, as in the Arabic text (Enger, p. 12), قوراكس.

[n] *i. e.* the youngest of the disciples.

[o] B. "and did not find it, he wrote."

[p] It is evident from the context that a leaf must have been lost in the manuscript from which our codex A. was copied. The Arabic text, too,

whole people, and offered incense, and passed the night at the shrine of Mār John, and prayed and said: "Our Lord Jesus the Messiah, Son of the glorious God, who didst love Mār John the apostle more than his fellows, if it be pleasing to Thy Godhead that all Thy wonders and glorious deeds, which Thou didst before my Lady Mary who bore Thee, should be revealed unto the world, let the apostle Mār John appear to us, conversing with us this night." And the brethren fell upon their faces praying, and became drowsy and slept. And Mār John the apostle stood beside these brethren and said to them: "Be not grieved, ye blessed, for the Messiah will reward you for all your wanderings.[q] Rise, take the book of the mother of my Lord, for lo, it is with me; and go to Mount Sinai, and ask after the welfare of our brethren, and say to them: 'John has sent you this book in order that there may be a commemoration of my Lady Mary three times in the year, because, if mankind celebrate her memory, they shall be delivered from wrath.'" This sign we saw, and trembled and were alarmed and in great fear. And the blessed one departed from beside us; and we were bowing down and praying. And the morning rose, and the verger (παρα-μονάριος) opened the door, and entered (the place) where the grace[r]

---

shows that, on the receipt of the bishop's letter, two monks were sent *from Mount Sinai to Ephesus*, and that it was they who assembled the whole people, and offered incense, and passed the night in prayer at the shrine of St. John (see Enger, p. 14): فلمّا وصل الكتابُ الي طور

سينا كتبوا لوقتهم الي اساقفة الرومية والاسكندرية من اجلها علي يَدَيْ رسّلٍ. قاصدين فطلبوها عندهم فلم يَجِدوها فارسلوا الي افسس رجلَيْن فلمّا وصلوا قاموا بالليل فضعوا (read يَضَعوا) البخور لوالدة سيّدنا يسوع المسيح [قاٮلين يا سيّدنا يسوع المسيح] انت الذي اخترتَ يوحنّا السليح النخ

[q] *Lit.* "will give the reward of your feet, as much as ye have walked in the countries."

[r] The Arabic has (Enger, p. 14), وكان ڡ كنيسة يوحنّا ڡي افسس

موضعًا (read موضعٌ) يّقَصَد ويّتبارَكُ منه ويّنبَع بَركةً ويّعطي بها الشفاءَ لمَن ياتيه علي اسمه. See the passages quoted by Tischendorf,

of Mār John flows; and there he found a written volume, placed upon the mouth of the spot whence the grace flows. And he took it up, and came forth before the whole people, and opened it, and found that it was written in Hebrew and Greek and Latin. And there was written in it thus: "This Jesus the Messiah, who was born of Mary, He is God in heaven and on earth." And this volume was translated* from Greek into Syriac at Ephesus; and was written out and sent[t] to Mount Sinai; and from Mount Sinai it was transcribed and sent[u] to Jerusalem. May our Lord Jesus the Messiah, who came from His holy heaven and performed the obsequies of His mother with great glory, let the rods of anger pass away from the face of the world, and make concord and peace reign over all mankind, for ever and ever, Amen. End of the First Book.

BOOK SECOND.

In the year 345,[v] in the month of the latter Teshrīn, my Lady Mary came forth from her house, and went to the tomb of the Messiah; because day by day she used to go and weep there.[w] But the Jews, as soon as the Messiah was dead,[x] closed the tomb, and heaped up large stones against its door; and set watchmen over the tomb and Golgotha, and gave them orders that, if any one should go and pray by the grave or on Golgotha, he should straightway die. And the Jews took the cross of our Lord, and the other two crosses, and the spear with which our Saviour had been pierced, and the nails which they had fixed in his hands and feet, and the robes of mockery which he had worn, and hid them; because they were afraid lest perchance one of the kings or princes should come and ask con-

---

Acta Apostolorum Apocrypha, proleg., p. lxxiv., from the writings of Augustine and Ephraim Theopolitanus. The latter writer, as cited by Photius, says regarding St. John: κατατεθεὶς γάρ, φασί, κατὰ τὴν αὐτοῦ ἐκείνου προτροπὴν ἔν τινι τόπῳ, ζητηθεὶς αἰφνίδιον οὐχ εὑρίσκετο, ἀλλὰ μόνον τὸ ἁγίασμα βρύον ἐξ αὐτοῦ τοῦ τόπου ἐν ᾧ πρὸς βραχεῖαν ῥοπὴν ἐτέθη. ἀφ' οὗ πάντες ὡς ἁγιάσμου πηγὴν τὸ ἅγιον ἐκεῖνο μύρον ἀρυόμεθα. The word ﻟﻴﺴﺎ is explained by Assemani (in Mai's *Scriptorum Veterum Nova Collectio*, tom. v., codd. Syr. Vat. Assem., p. 21) to mean "pulvis loci, ubi martyres coronati fuerunt, quem oleo et aqua dilutum ad extremam unctionem adhibent."

  [t] *Lit.* "went forth."   [t] *Lit.* "went."   [u] *Lit.* "came."
  [v] Of the Seleucian or Greek era, A.D. 33 or 34.
  [w] See Enger, p. 18.
  [x] B. adds on the margin, "and had risen from the grave."

cerning the slaying of the Messiah. And the watchmen came
in and said to the priests: "Mary comes in the evening and the
morning and prays there." And there was a commotion in
Jerusalem concerning my Lady Mary; and the priests went to
the judge and said to him: "My lord, send and order Mary
not to go and pray at the grave and Golgotha."

Whilst they were deliberating, lo, letters came from Abgar,[y]
king of the city of Urhāi (Edessa), to Sabinus the procurator
(ἐπίτροπος), who had been appointed by the emperor Tiberius,
and whose jurisdiction extended as far as the river Euphrates.
Because Addai the apostle, one of the seventy-two apostles,
had gone down and built a church at Urhāi, and healed the
disease of king Abgar; for king Abgar loved Jesus the Messiah
and asked at all times concerning Him; and when the Messiah
was dead, and king Abgar heard that the Jews had killed Him
on the cross, he was much grieved. And Abgar arose, and
rode, and came to the river Euphrates, and wished to go up
against Jerusalem and lay it waste. And when Abgar came
and reached the river Euphrates, he reflected in his mind, "If
I cross over, there will be enmity between me and the emperor
Tiberius." And Abgar wrote letters and sent them to the
procurator Sabinus, and Sabinus sent them to the emperor
Tiberius. Thus wrote Abgar to the emperor Tiberius. "From
Abgar, king of the city of Urhāi, much peace to thy Majesty,
our Lord Tiberius. That thy sovereignty might not be dis-
paraged in my sight, I have not crossed the river Euphrates;
for I was wishing to go up against Jerusalem and lay it waste,
because it slew the Messiah, the wise Physician. But do thou,
like a great king, as thou bearest sway over the whole earth
and over us, send and do me justice on the people of Jerusalem.
For let thy Majesty know, that I wish thee to do me justice on
the crucifiers." And Sabinus received the letters and sent them
to the emperor Tiberius. And when he had read them, the
emperor Tiberius was very much enraged, and was going to
destroy and kill all the Jews.

And the people of Jerusalem heard (this), and were alarmed;[z]
and the priests went to the Hēgemōn and said to him: "My
lord, send and order Mary not to go to pray at the tomb and
Golgotha." The judge said to the priests: "Go ye, and order
her, and admonish her what ye please." And the priests went
to my Lady Mary and said to her: "The judge orders thee not
to go and pray at the tomb and Golgotha; and now, Mary, we
say unto thee, Remember the sins thou hast committed before

God, and do not lead people astray, and say that he who was born of thee is the Messiah. Heaven and earth testify that he is the son of Joseph the carpenter. If then thou wishest to pray, enter into the synagogue and hear the laws of Moses, and we will call unto God and He will have mercy upon thee. But if thou dost not agree to these things, depart from Jerusalem and go to thy house at Bethlehem, for we will not permit thee to pray at the tomb and Golgotha." These things the Jews said to my Lady Mary, and she did not agree to them. Afterwards my Lady Mary fell sick; and she sent and called all the women of the quarter in which she dwelt,[a] and said to them: "Fare ye well, for I am going to Bethlehem, to the house which I have there; because the Jews will not permit me to pray at the tomb and on the Golgotha of the Messiah. But whoever of you wishes, let her come with me to Bethlehem; for I place my trust in my Master[b] whom I have in heaven, who, whenever I cry to Him, hears me." And when my Lady Mary had said to the daughters of Jerusalem that whoever wished should go with her, the virgins who ministered unto her drew near and said to her: "Whoever wishes to go with thee, my Lady Mary, shall receive a blessing from God. But we will not leave thee till we die, for for thy sake we have left our parents and our brothers and all that we have, and have come with thee to minister unto thee; and with thee we wish to die, and with thee we wish to live."

These virgins were the daughters of rich men and rulers of Jerusalem. Their names were these: Callĕtha, and Neshrā, and Tābĕthā.[c] Callĕthā was the daughter of Mār Nicodemus, the friend of the Messiah; and by the name of Callĕthā (the bride) is designated the glorious Church, the betrothed of the Messiah. And the second, whose name was Neshrā, was the daughter of Gamaliel, the chief of the synagogue of the Jews; and by the likeness of Neshrā (the eagle) is symbolized the king Messiah, who on His wings carries and bears aloft the holy church, which is betrothed unto Him from before the foundations of the world. And she, whose name was Tābĕthā, was the daughter of Tobia, a man of comitian rank (κομητιάνος). This Tobia was one of the people of the house of king Archelaus; and Archelaus was of the family of Nero Caesar, he who crucified Simon the

---

[a] See Enger, p. 26 and p. 29.

[b] ܪܒܘܠܝ, *Rabbūlī*, a corruption of ܪܒܘܢܝ, *Rabbūnī*, רבּוני.

[c] See Enger, p. 30, where the names are كنة, دو رفعة, and نعمة.

Of these the first is a corruption of كَلَّ, and the third a translation of the Syriac name. The second seems to be corrupt.

chief of the apostles.   The interpretation of these names is this.
Callĕthā is the Catholic (Church), which is in the heavenly
Jerusalem; and this church, that we have on earth, is the likeness of that which is in heaven, and on it is established the
throne of the glorious God.   And Neshrā is the Messiah, who
sits at the right hand of His Father on the throne of the
Seraphim.   And Tābĕthā is the Holy Spirit, by whom life is
given to all men.   These were the names of the virgins who
ministered unto my Lady Mary.   And these virgins arose along
with my Lady Mary, and went forth to Bethlehem on Thursday,
and passed the night at Bethlehem.

And on that Friday my Lady Mary was distressed,[d] and
said to them: "Bring nigh unto me the censer of incense, for
I wish to pray to my Master whom I have in heaven."   And
they brought nigh unto her the censer of incense; and she
prayed and said: "My Master, the Messiah, whom I have in
heaven, hear the voice of Thy parent, and send to me Mār
John the young, whose blessing is great, that I may see him
and rejoice; and send to me the apostles his fellows, that I may
see them and praise Thy grace which aids me; and Thou hearest
me as soon as I pray unto Thee."

And when the blessed one prayed thus, John was in Ephesus,
alive.[e]   And he went forth to go to the church of Ephesus, and
the Holy Spirit said to him: "The time draws nigh that the
mother of thy Lord should depart from the world.   Go to
Bethlehem to salute her."   These things spake the Holy
Spirit to John; and John went out from Ephesus to go to
Bethlehem, and prostrated himself to pray, and said: "Our
Lord Jesus the Messiah, give strength to my feet that I may go
quickly to Bethlehem, on account of what the Holy Spirit made
known to me."   Thus prayed John, and a cloud of light snatched
him away, and brought him to the door of the upper chamber
in Bethlehem.   And John opened the door of the upper chamber, and entered, and found the blessed one lying on the bed;
and he kissed her on her breast and on her knees, and cried out
and said to her: "Peace be unto thee, thou mother of my Lord!
peace be unto thee, thou mother of God!   Be not grieved that
with great glory thou are departing from this world."   And my
Lady Mary rejoiced much that Mār John had come to her.   My
Lady Mary says to him: "Set forth the censer of incense, and
pray."   And Mār John set forth the censer of incense and
prayed; and there was a voice from heaven saying: "Amen;
be assembled, all of ye."   And John listened and heard this

---

[d] See Enger, p. 30.   [e] Ibid., p. 32.

voice, that cried out in heaven; and the Holy Spirit said to John: "Hast thou heard this voice, which cried out in heaven?" John said: "I have heard it." - The Holy Spirit said: "This voice is a messenger to the apostles thy fellows, who are coming here to-day." And John continued praying, and the Holy Spirit made known to the apostles, wherever they were, that they should sit upon decorated steeds and on clouds of light, and go to Bethlehem to the blessed one.

To Simon Cephas*f* It made this known in Rome, as he was going in to offer the oblation in the church where was the oblation of strangers; and he was lying prostrate and praying before the altar; and the Holy Spirit said to him: "The time draws nigh that the mother of thy Lord should depart from this world; go to Bethlehem to salute her."

And the Holy Spirit informed Paul in the city called Tiberias. It found Paul as he was contending with the Jews, who were striving with him, and reviling him, and saying to him: "Thy words are not received, which thou utterest concerning the Messiah. Because thou art from Tarsus, and the son of a harness-maker,*g* and the child of poor people, thou takest the name of the Messiah (in thy mouth), and goest about with it!" And the Holy Spirit said to him: "The time draws nigh that the mother of thy Lord should depart from this world; go to Bethlehem to greet her."

And the Holy Spirit informed Thomas in India, who had gone in to visit the nephew of Lūdān,*h* the king of India. And he was sitting by his bed and talking to him; and the Holy Spirit said to him: "The time draws nigh for the mother of thy Lord to leave this world; go to Bethlehem to greet her."

And the Holy Spirit informed Matthew, (saying:) "The time draws nigh for the mother of thy Lord to leave this world; go to Bethlehem to greet her." And Matthew was at Yābūs.*i*

---

f See Enger, p. 38.

g Thomas à Novaria (or rather Elias of Nisibis), *Thesaurus Arabico-Syro-Latinus,* p. 106, Ephippiarius, كمكاز, سرَاج; MS. dictionary, Add. 7203, سراج اكمكز, *i. e.,* سرَاج, *a maker of saddles.* The word seems to be derived from the Latin *lorarius.*

h *Or* Laudān, Gr. τοῦ βασιλέως ὀνόματι Λαβδανούς (var. Κλαυδανούς).

i Farther on, Matthew is said to have been on board of a ship (Gr. ἐν πλοίῳ). As the writer makes use of other Scriptural names without much judgment (*e. g. Jochébed* and *Jephunneh*), it is possible that he has here employed the name of *Jebūs,* יבוס, without any regard to geographical propriety.

And the Holy Spirit informed James in Jerusalem, (saying:) "The time draws nigh for the mother of your Lord to leave this world; go to Bethlehem to greet her."

And the Holy Spirit informed Bartholomew[j] in the Thebais, (saying:) "The time draws nigh for the mother of your Lord to depart from this world; go to Bethlehem to greet her."

Now none of the disciples were dead as yet, except Andrew, the brother of Simon Cephas, and Philip, and Luke, and Simon the Cananite; these were dead.[k] And on that day the Holy Spirit informed them in their graves, (saying:) "Rise from Sheōl." And the Holy Spirit said unto them: "Do not suppose that the resurrection is come; but your rising to-day from your graves is wholly that ye may go to greet the mother of your Lord, for the time draws nigh for her to leave the world."

And the Holy Spirit informed Mark, (saying:) "The time draws nigh for the mother of your Lord to leave the world; go to Bethlehem to greet her."

These things did the Holy Spirit make known to the holy apostles. And while the apostles were wondering in the countries where they were, how they should get to Bethlehem to my Lady Mary, their Lord sent to them chariots; and a cloud of light descended and snatched away Peter, and he was standing between heaven and earth, and waiting for the apostles his fellows to come to him. And straightway the Holy Spirit snatched away all the apostles on chariots, and they came to Peter. And terrible winds blew,[l] and heaven and earth shone with a strong light. And the disciples set upon eleven[m] thrones, and the thrones were placed on chariots, and the Holy Spirit guided these chariots, and they came between heaven and earth; and the apostles arrived at Bethlehem.

And the Holy Spirit informed John, (saying:) "Go out and receive the apostles thy fellows, who are come." And John went out and bowed down to them. Peter said to him: "Is the mother of our Lord dead, my brother John?" John said: "She is not yet dead." And the apostles went in to the upper chamber to my Lady Mary, and kissed her on her breast and on her knees, and stood up before her and said to her: "Fear not, thou blessed one, and be not grieved. The Lord God who was born of thee, He removes thee from this world with glory to the glorious mansions of the blessed God, over which thy Son rules, and in which He gladdens the just who love Him." And my Lady Mary raised herself and sat up on the bed, and said to the

---

[j] The MSS. have here merely *Tolmai* instead of *Bar Tolmai*.
[k] See Enger, p. 38.   [l] Ibid., p. 40.   [m] B. "twelve."

apostles:[n] "Now I am certain that my Master will come from heaven, and I shall see Him, and afterwards I shall die, as ye are come and I have seen you. And now I wish you to tell me, who informed you that I was dying, and from what regions ye are come to me, that your coming was so quick. Reveal to me and inform me, because I know of a truth that He who was born of me is the Son of the living God, and I worship Him, because, according to the lowliness of His handmaid, so hath He dealt with me." Peter said to the apostles his fellows: "Let every one of you tell the blessed one how the Holy Spirit spoke to him, and whence he came."

John said: "To me in Ephesus the Holy Spirit announced it and said: 'The time draws nigh for the mother of your Lord to leave the world; go to Bethlehem to greet her.' And a cloud of light snatched me away and brought me to the door of the upper chamber."

Peter said: "To me in Rome the Holy Spirit announced it on the morning of Thursday, and said to me: 'The time draws nigh for the mother of your Lord to leave the world; go to Bethlehem to greet her.' And a cloud of light snatched me away, and I stood between heaven and earth, and saw the chariots of all the apostles, which were flying and coming to me."

Paul said: "I was in the city called Tiberias, and the Jews were disputing with me there. And the Holy Spirit said to me: "The time draws nigh for the mother of your Lord to leave this world; go to Bethlehem to greet her.' And a cloud of light snatched me away and brought me to you."

Thomas said: "I was informed in India, when I had gone in to visit the nephew of Lūdān, the king of India; and as I was talking to him, the Holy Spirit said to me: 'The time draws nigh for the mother of thy Lord to leave this world.' And a cloud of light snatched me away and brought me to you."

Mark said: "I was performing the service of the third hour, and as. I was praying, a cloud of light snatched me away and brought me to you."

James said: "I was in Jerusalem, and was sitting in the church of Sion, and we were gathering together some of the vessels of the Lord's house.[o] And a little before, I had gone

---

[n] See Enger, p. 40.

[o] I am doubtful about the meaning of this passage, but have followed Bar Bablūl, who explains ܟ̈ܦܐ by ܚ̈ܢܡ and ܡ̈ܢܦ. The words may, however, be also translated: "were wrapping up some of the vessels of the Lord's house," viz., after they had been used at divine service.

out from Jerusalem towards Bethlehem, and the Holy Spirit came in unto me and said to me: 'The time draws nigh for the mother of thy Lord to leave the world; go to Bethlehem to greet her.' And a cloud of light snatched me away and brought me unto you."

Matthew said: "I have given and am giving glory to God; for when I was sitting in a ship, storms arose against me to destroy the ship; and a cloud of light snatched me away and brought me to you."

Philip said: "I was dead and laid in the grave; and I heard a voice, which called me, (saying:) 'Philip, rise thence.' And a cloud of light snatched me away and brought me to you."

Simon the Cananite said: "I too am risen from the grave. I saw a right hand which laid hold of me, and it raised me up from the abode of the dead, where I was lying among them; and a cloud of light snatched me away and brought me to you."

Luke said: "I too am risen from the grave. There struck on my ears as it were the sound of a seraph's trumpet, and a light shone through the whole grave in which I was lying, and I thought that the resurrection had arrived. And a cloud of light snatched me away and brought me to you."

Andrew answered and said: "I too am risen from the grave. The voice of the Son of God struck on my ears and said to me: 'Andrew, arise, go with thy fellows to Bethlehem, and I will come to you with the bands of the angels; for the time is come in which the holy Mary shall be crowned (and depart) from the world.' And a cloud of light snatched me away and brought me to you."

Bartholomew said: "I was in Thebais, and was preaching of the grace and peace of our Lord Jesus the Messiah; and I saw the Holy Spirit coming like lightning from heaven; and a cloud of light snatched me away and brought me to you."

So spake the holy apostles before my Lady Mary, and each of them told how he had come to her. And when my Lady Mary heard these things from the holy apostles, she stretched out her hands to heaven and prayed, and answered and said:ᴾ "I worship and praise and glorify (God), that I am not a mockery to the nations of the Gentiles, and that the words of the Jews have not turned out true, who said that they would burn me when I was dead. But I believe that He who was born of me is the ruler of heaven and earth." And after the blessed one prayed, the apostles set forth the censer of incense and

ᴾ See Enger, p. 42.

prayed there. And it thundered like the sound of wheels rolling over the surface of the sky, and a voice like that of a man was heard in the midst of the chariot of seraphs who were standing over the chamber of the blessed one. And the people of Bethlehem went in and told the judge and the priests of Jerusalem all that they saw and all that they heard. End of the second book.

Book Third.

And certain men of Bethlehem, when they saw the signs which were done, came to the house of the blessed one.[q] And the people of Bethlehem saw the disciples when they came and were ministering in the upper chamber; and they saw the clouds coming and dropping down a gentle dew on all Bethlehem; and they saw the sun and moon, which came and worshipped before the upper chamber; and they saw the stammering, and dumb, and blind, and deaf, and sick, and afflicted, and those who had evil spirits, and every one who had a pain, going to her and being healed. And women were coming to her[r] from the cities and regions and from Rome and Athens, the daughters of kings and procurators and prefects, and bringing presents and offerings, and they were coming and worshipping my Lady Mary, and every one who had a pain, and she was curing them.

There came to my Lady Mary a woman from Bērȳtus (Beirūt), who had a devil, that at all times was strangling her; and the blessed one prayed over her and cursed these devils in the name of our Lord Jesus the Messiah, and straightway the devils came out of her.

And there came to her Yūchabar (Jochébed) from Alexandria, the daughter of Nonnus the hyparch, who was completely covered with[s] leprosy. And she came and prostrated herself before my Lady Mary, and she took water and made the sign of the cross over it, and sprinkled it on her, and she was healed.

And there came to her Abigáil from Egypt, who had the affliction of strangury; and she prayed over her and she was healed.

And there came to her Flavia from Thessalonīca, whose right eye Satan had destroyed, and she made the sign of the cross over it, and she was cured.

And there came to her Malchū, the daughter of Sabinus,

---

who had two devils, one that tormented her by night and another that came upon her by day; and she prayed over her, and she was healed.

And there was a great festival in Jerusalem, and there came to it many people. And the sick and afflicted, who came to Jerusalem, asked, "Where is my Lady Mary?" And they said, "At Bethlehem." And persons without number went forth and came to Bethlehem. And those who were afflicted were crying and saying: "My Lady Mary, mother of God, have mercy upon us." And my Lady Mary heard the voice of the persons who were crying to her, and she prayed and said: "Our Lord Jesus the Messiah, do Thou hear the voice of the souls that cry to Thee." And the virtue of help went forth from my Lady Mary upon the afflicted, and straightway two thousand six hundred[*] souls were healed, men and women and children. And there was great thanksgiving on that day, because, as soon as they were cured, these sick went to the praetorium, and told to the judge and the priests all that my Lady Mary did by her prayers. And they disturbed the priests and the Hēgemōn, and they (*i. e.*, the priests) said to him : "Order this woman not to remain either at Bethlehem or in the jurisdiction of Jerusalem." The judge said: "I have no power to send and drive a woman out of her house." They said to him : "Send men with staves, and let them bring to us the disciples and Mary." And after they cried saying: "By the life of Tiberius, if thou dost not do our pleasure, we will make it known to him," the judge ordered a captain of a thousand to go, he and thirty men with him,[*] to Bethlehem, and to bring Mary and the disciples. And they set out and went. And the Holy Spirit revealed it to the apostles, (saying:) "Lo, men are coming against you from Jerusalem. Rise, go hence, and fear not; I will carry you and make you pass through the air of heaven over the heads of the men who are coming against you; for the power of the adored Son is with you." And the apostles arose, and carried the bed of my Lady Mary, and went forth from the upper chamber, and passed over the heads of the men who were coming against them, and they did not see them. When these men arrived at Bethlehem, and opened the door of the upper chamber and entered, and found nothing in it,— neither the disciples nor my Lady Mary,—they were very angry, and seized the people of Bethlehem and said to them : "Will ye

---

[*] See Enger, p. 50, where the Arabic text has 2800. By an oversight Enger has written on p. 51, "duo millia et *octoginta*."

[*] See Enger, p. 52, where the Arabic text has " 30,000 horse and foot" ! The Greek has merely ἀποστέλλει χιλίαρχον.

not come in and say to the judge and the priests, ' We have found nothing there'?" And the people of Bethlehem went in along with these men and said : " We have found nothing there." And the priests said : " These disciples of the seducer have made some incantations and blinded your eyes, and ye have not seen them." The judge said to the people of Bethlehem : " If ye hear any news of them again anywhere, seize them and bring to us."

And after five days, the angels of the Lord were seen, entering into and going out of Jerusalem to my Lady Mary.* And people assembled from many quarters (of the city), and cried out and said: "Holy virgin, mother of God, beseech the Messiah, whom thou hast in heaven, to send us healing, for we are afflicted." And the priests assembled and stood up and cried at the praetorium : " Illustrious judge, there will be a great uproar concerning this woman." The judge said to them : " What shall I do for you?" They said to him : " Let us take fire, and go and burn the house in which she dwells." The Hēgemōn said : " Do what you please." And the people of Jerusalem came and took fire and wood, and went to the house in which the blessed one dwelt; and the judge was standing at a distance and looking on. And when they came to the house, the doors were closed. And when they laid hands on them to break them down, straightway an angel dashed his wings in their faces, and fire blazed forth from the doors without any one casting it; and the faces and hair of the persons who came up to the door of the house were burned, and many people died there. And there was great fear upon all Jerusalem. But the judge, when he saw this sight, that fire blazed forth from the door without any one casting it, stretched out his hands to heaven and cried and said : "Of a truth this deed which I have seen is (that) of the Son of the living God, who was born of the Virgin Mary and is worshipped and glorified by the angels and archangels, and in it he is worshipped and glorified." And when the judge had done speaking these words, he gave orders that next day he should send and bring the people of Jerusalem, the priests and elders and Sadducees. And the judge said to them: "Ye wicked nation, nation that crucified God, I know that ye are men bitter of soul and stiff of neck, doers of the wish of your own heart. But I thank God that I am not of your country nor one of your communion. And now, people of Jerusalem, I give orders that not one of you is to go near the house of this holy (woman)." Then drew near Caleb, the chief of the Sadducees,ʷ who believed

---

* See Enger, p. 54, at the foot.   ʷ Ibid., p. 58.

in the Messiah and in my Lady Mary the blessed; and he drew near to the judge, and whispered to him saying: "My Lord, let thy Highness make them swear by this oath which I tell thee, for to this oath they cannot play false. Make them swear thus: 'By God who brought up Israel out of the land of Egypt, and by the holy books of the law, (so and so will I do unto you,) if ye do not tell me how ye call the child of Mary. Do ye call him a prophet? Do ye account him a righteous man? Is he the Messiah, the Son of God? Is he a man of the sons of men?'" And when the judge had called the people of Jerusalem and the priests and elders, and made them swear by the God of Israel, and by the holy books of the law, (he said:) "Let every man who believes on my Lady Mary and on the child who was born of her, that he is the Messiah, the Son of God, separate himself and stand by himself; and let him who does not believe, shew himself as an unbeliever." Then the people were divided into two parties, and those who believed separated themselves on one side.ᶻ The Hēgemōn said to those who believed in the Messiah, "What say ye? Do ye believe in this child, who was born of Mary?" They said to him: "We believe in him, that he is the Messiah, the Son of the living God, and He it is who by His command rules heaven and earth." The unbelievers said to the Hēgemōn: "My Lord, according to our books, the Messiah is not yet come." The judge said to them: "Tell me; this one who is come, what reckon ye him?" They said to him: "He is a seducer, who is not good like one of the righteous." But the judge was praying in his mind to God, that those who believed in the Messiah might gain the victory.

The lovers of the Messiah said to the unbelievers: "Do ye show the miracles and signs which the ancient and the middle and the latter (prophets) have done, and we will show the signs which the Messiah did, that they are more than all created things."

The unbelievers said: "Whence show ye to us that the son of Mary is the Messiah?"

The lovers of the Messiah: "We are showing it."

The Hēgemōn said to them: "Not with clamour nor uproar are ye to utter your words against one another; but speak to one another with a gentle voice according to your books, for I too wish to see and know what are your doctrines."

The lovers of the Messiah said to the unbelievers: "Our father Adam, when dying, commanded in his testament his son Seth and said to him: 'My son Seth, lo, offerings are laid by

---

ᶻ See Enger, p. 60.

me in the cave of treasures, gold and myrrh and frankincense; because God is about to come into the world, and to be seized by evil and wicked men, and to die and make by his death a resurrection for all the children of Adam.' And lo, the Magi, the sons of kings, came carrying these offerings, and went and conveyed them to the Son of God, who was born of the Virgin Mary in Bethlehem. We are not ashamed of anything we say. What say ye?"

The unbelievers said: "Is the Messiah, pray, more excellent than Abraham in the sight of God, who opened heaven and spake to him as we speak to one another?"

The lovers of the Messiah said to the unbelievers: "Ye see that ye know nothing. For we, who are lovers of the Messiah, know that it is the Son of Mary who created Adam; and whilst Abraham was not yet formed in his mother's womb, the Messiah was before all created things. And as for what ye say, that God spake with Abraham from heaven, it was the Messiah who spake with him."

The unbelievers said: "Is the Messiah, pray, of whom ye are so proud, better than Isaac, who became an offering, and the savour of his offering went up and pleased God above in the supernal heights, and heaven and earth were delighted with it?"

The lovers of the Messiah said: "That Isaac was not slain on the altar, when Abraham offered him, was entirely because the Messiah, who was to be born of Mary, was about to come and die for all creatures, and by his death the whole world was to be delivered from error. Isaac, if he had died, would have been called a single victim; but when the Messiah died, an offering of all created things was offered in Him to God."

The unbelievers said: "Is the Messiah, pray, more excellent than Jacob, who went up and slept on the mount of Gilead; and God opened the heavens and spake with him, and stretched a ladder from heaven to earth, and the angels too descended to salute him?"

The lovers of the Messiah said: "Jacob, and the angels, and the ladder which he saw, pointed to the coming of the Messiah and the mystery of His death."

The unbelievers said: "The ascent of Elias to heaven puts you to shame, for all that he says in heaven is heard, and all that he wills on earth is done."

The lovers of the Messiah said to the unbelievers: "Elias went up in a whirlwind to this heaven, in which are fixed the sun and moon, and no man worshipped him in his ascent, except Elisha his disciple. But the Messiah, who went up to heaven, went up not to one heaven, but above all the heavens; and when the Messiah went up to heaven, all creatures above and below bowed their heads and worshipped him, and lo, they worship and glorify him for ever."

The unbelievers said: "Let Moses come and his signs, by which he tormented the Egyptians and delivered Israel. And notwithstanding that Pharaoh wish to restrain us from reaching the sea, Moses took the dry staff that was in his hand and piled up with it the waves of the sea in heaps."

The lovers of the Messiah said: "Jesus too, who was born of Mary, rebuked devils and they were scattered before Him. And to Simon Peter, when the sea was going to swallow him up, He stretched out His hand, and raised him up, and he did not sink. And if the Messiah had not power over sea and land and all created things, whence would all these created things obey Him when He orders them?"

Then the judge commanded, and four[v] men of the unbelievers were severely scourged. And the day declined, and the Hēgemōn passed the night in his prætorium in great wrath. And when the cock crew, the judge went forth, he and his two young men and his son with him, who had a disease of the stomach and the strangury. And he knocked at the door of the blessed one, and her damsel came out and answered him. The Hēgemōn said to her: "Go in and tell thy mistress that the judge of the city of Jerusalem wishes to worship her." And my Lady Mary ordered that the door should be opened for him; and he entered and knelt down and worshipped her, and cried aloud and said to her: "Hail to thee, mother of God! and hail to the Messiah, who was born of thee! Hail to the heavens, that bear the throne of the Godhead of thy Son! The Son, the Messiah, who arose from thee,—mouth and tongue are too feeble to narrate the glories of thee and of thy Son, the holy child. The earth on which thou walkest shall become a heaven; the heaven that beholds thee shall give a blessing to the human beings that believe in thee; the whole that see thee shall be gladdened; the sick that come unto thee, thou shalt give them healing. I worship thee, my Lady Mary. Stretch out thy right hand and bless me, me and this the only child which God has given me; and pray for the souls whom I have in the city of Rome, that I may go in peace and see them, and carry presents and offerings, and come and worship thee." Now my Lady Mary was standing and praying, and the censer of incense was set before her. And when she heard the words of the Hēgemōn, she turned round and prayed, and stretched out her hands and blessed him

---

[v] A later hand has altered *four* into *forty*, and such too is the reading of the Arabic text. See Enger, p. 63.

and his son, and said to him, "Sit down." Now the twelve disciples of our Lord were there with my Lady Mary. And when she said to the judge, "Sit down," he did not wish to sit, but ran and fell straightway at the feet of the apostles, and said to them : "Peace be with you, ye chosen ones, who have been chosen of God before all creatures ! and hail to the Messiah, who chose you to be his Heralds in the world !" The apostles said to him : "We have heard what thou hast done to the crucifiers, and have prayed much for thee." The judge said to them : "Enough for them is the scorn they are become before God and men." The apostles said to him ; "What have they done, that they should not be a scorn ?" So spake the apostles to the Hēgemōn, when he went and worshipped them. And he was dismissed, and went forth from Jerusalem, and came to the city of Rome to his house, on account of what had happened. And when he went to Rome,* he went in to the emperors and the great, and narrated the miracles and wonders which my Lady Mary was doing in the world. And the disciples of Paul and Peter too, whom they had in the city of Rome, went and wrote these holy words which they heard from the Hēgemōn.

And their disciples wrote to the apostles, (saying :)ª "When ye have performed the obsequies of the blessed one, bring with you to the city of Rome the book of her decease, how she departed from this world; for lo, all places are full of the praises of the blessed one, and since we have believed in her here, she has often appeared to the human beings who believe in her prayers. For she appeared here on the sea, when it was agitated and swollen and going to destroy the ships that were sailing on it. And the sailors called on her name and said, 'My Lady Mary, mother of God, have mercy on us;' and she rose upon them like the sun, and delivered these ships, which were ninety-two in number, and saved them from destruction, and not one of them was lost. And she appeared by day, at the momentᵇ when robbers had fallen upon certain men and were going to slay them; and these men cried and said, 'My Lady Mary, mother of God, have mercy on us;' and she rose upon them like (a flash of) lightning, and rescued these men, and they suffered no harm. And she appeared to a widow woman, whose son went to look into a well of water, and fell into it; and there was no one near to bring him up. And the woman cried out at the mouth of the well and said, 'My Lady Mary, mother of God, have

---

* See Enger, p. 68.   ª Ibid., p. 96.

ᵇ I have translated as if the reading were ܒܛܘܪܐ ; but the text has ܒܛܘܪܐ, "on a mountain."

mercy on me.' And my Lady Mary appeared to her, and snatched up the child, and he was not drowned; and she gave him to his mother alive. And she appeared to a man who was sick for sixteen years, and the physicians were not able to give him any help all this length of years. Then he brought a censer, and cast into it incense, and bethought him of my Lady Mary and said, 'My Lady Mary, mother of God, heal me.' And straightway she came to him and healed him, and sent him to the church of Rome before all the people. And she appeared to a merchant, who borrowed a thousand dīnārs *(aurei)*, and went to trade with them in another place. And he was going along the road, and the purse dropped from him and was lost. And after he had journeyed a long time, he sat down to eat bread, and turned over his clothes and sought for the purse and could not find it. And he was weeping and crying, and coming along the road and praying, 'My Lady Mary, mother of God, have mercy on me.' Then my Lady Mary had mercy on him, and took him and made him stand over the purse of dīnārs, and he took what was his and missed nothing. And she appeared on the way to Egypt to two women, against whom there came out a large snake and ran after them to devour them. And they called on her name and said : 'My Lady Mary, mother of God, have mercy on us.' And my Lady Mary appeared to them, and smote the snake on its mouth, and it was split in two ; and these women were delivered and did not perish."

Whilst my Lady Mary was doing these miracles at Rome and in all countries, the apostles were beside her. And whilst the apostles and my Lady Mary were at Jerusalem, the Holy Spirit said to them :[c] "To morrow morning take my Lady Mary and go out from Jerusalem by the road that leads to the head of the valley. Lo, there are there three caves and a raised seat[d] of clay. Take in and place the blessed one on that seat, and minister unto her until I tell ye." And at the time of morning the apostles arose, and took up the blessed one, and went forth from Jerusalem; and the Jews were standing and mocking and saying to one another: "Lo, the disciples of the seducer are bearing Mary and going ;" and the blessed one was looking upon them. And there was there a powerful[e] Jew,

---

[c] See Enger, p. 70.

[d] ܡܨܛܒ݁ܐ=مصطبة or رَكْو, which latter Enger has wrongly trans-lated by "locus arenosus."

[e] For جبان in the Arabic text read جَبَّار, חזק. The word for "timid, cowardly," is جَبَان, without *teshdīd*.

whose name was Yūphanyā*f* (Jephunneh), who was tall and of a
fine figure and immense strength. To him the scribes of Israel
said : "Come near, Yūphanyā, and (only) blow upon Mary,
and she will fall from her bed (*or* litter) ; for lo, the disciples of
the seducer think that they have prevailed over Jerusalem."
And Yūphanyā went and cast his two arms upon the two poles
(*or* handles)*g* of the bed, and hung on by them, in order that
the bed might be broken and fall down, and that the Jews
might carry it off and burn it with fire. Yūphanyā had laid
his hands upon the bed, and the angel of the Lord smote him
with a sword of fire and cut off his two arms from his shoulders,
and they hung like ropes on the bed. And he was weeping and
coming after the apostles who were carrying it ; and he cried
and said : "Our Lord Jesus the Messiah, have mercy on me !
Ye disciples of Jesus, have mercy on me !" The disciples said
to him : "Why callest thou on us? Call on my Lady Mary,—
on her whose bed thou wast wishing to break,—and she will
answer thee." Yūphanyā said : "My Lady Mary, mother of
God, have mercy on me !" And my Lady Mary said to Peter :
"Give to Yūphanyā his arms, which are hanging on the bed."
And when Peter had spat on one of them, he said : "In the
name of my Lady Mary, the mother of God, cleave to thy
place." Then Peter made these arms cleave to their places ; and
Peter took up a dry stick and gave it to him, and said to him :
"Go thou too and show the power of the Son of God to all the
Jews, and tell of my Lady Mary, what she hath done for thee
by her prayers ;" because the Jews greatly hated my Lady Mary,
and were also saying : "If, now that she is alive, she prevails over
us, when she is dead and we see where she is buried, we will go
and take her corpse and burn it with fire." But the Messiah,
who was born of the Virgin Mary, gathered His mother out of
this world from before the race of crucifiers, who were thirsting
after her like destroying wolves to devour her, the blessed sheep.
Let no one who loves God and my Lady Mary, who bore Him,
be a companion and friend of the Jews ; for if he is so, the love
of the Messiah is severed from him. Here ends the third book.

---

f The Arabic text has يوفيا, "Yūphiyā," a corruption of يوننيا,
Gr. 'Ιεφωνίας (var. 'Ιωφονίας).

g I do not remember to have met with the word اقصا elsewhere,
but the meaning is evidently that which I have given, viz. the two "poles"
or "handles," by means of which the litter was carried (rad. قصب).

BOOK FOURTH.

And when the apostles were ministering unto my Lady Mary in the cave, the Holy Spirit informed them, (saying :)[A] " In the sixth month the angel Gabriel was sent to the mother of your Lord, my Lady Mary, and saluted her, and announced to her concerning the Holy Child that was to be born of her for the salvation of the world, [and the sixth month is Nīsān,] on the first of Nīsān, as my Lady Mary was sitting, and there were lying before her dyed curtains[i] for the front of the door, which she was making for the house of the Lord." And again the Holy Spirit said to the apostles : " Thus believe and thus confess ; that on a Sunday your Lord was announced and came to the world ; and on a Sunday He was born in Bethlehem ; and on a Sunday the people of Jerusalem went forth unwillingly and glorified Him with hosannas heavenly and earthly ; and on a Sunday He rose from the grave, and put to shame all His cruci-fiers. And to-morrow again, which is a Sunday, He will come from heaven, with all created things, that are above and below, before Him, and will glorify the mother who bore Him, and those who did not believe in His coming to the world shall be put to shame."

And the Sabbath day (Saturday) declined, and the apostles and angels were ministering before her.[j] And the morning of the holy Sunday arose, and there came Eve, the mother of all human beings, and the mother of my Lady Mary, and Elisabeth the mother of St. John the Baptist. And the mother of my Lady Mary drew near, and placed her mouth on her breast, and kissed her and said to her : " Blessed be God, who chose thee for Himself, that thou mightest be a dwelling-place for His glory ; for from the time thou wast formed in my womb, I knew that the God of heaven would come and dwell in thee." And Peter drew near and moved aside these women, and they stood at the head of the bed[k] of my Lady Mary, because chariots were seen coming. 'And there came our father Adam, and Seth his son, and Shem and Noah, who was leaven to this world ; and they worshipped before the blessed one. And the chariots of the fathers appeared coming, of Abraham, Isaac, and Jacob,

---

[A] See Enger, p. 74.

[i] Add. 7203. المصبوغ الصوف ܪ̈ܘܚܟܠܐ, *i. e. sub'ānā* means *dyed wool*.

[j] See Enger, p. 76.

[k] Add. 7203. معذة راسه عند ܐܦ̇ܩ̣; Heb. מְרַאֲשֹׁתָיו.

and of Mār David the singer; and they worshipped before the glorious one.   And there appeared coming the chariots of the prophets, with censers in their hands, and they worshipped before the holy one.   And created beings without number came forth from the gate of heaven to descend to earth.   Then appeared the person of the Great King, coming and holding the sign of the cross in His hand; and He descended and stood beside her.   And all the created beings blessed and worshipped Him.   And our Lord called to His mother and said to her: "Mary."   And she said to Him, "Here I am, my Lord Rabbūlī;" which is, being interpreted, Teacher.   And my Lady Mary said to her Son: "Stretch out Thy hands and place them on my eyes, and bless me."   And the Messiah stretched out His hands and laid them on the eyes of His mother; and she took them and kissed them and said: "I worship these holy hands, which made heaven and earth."

Then the apostles drew near and said to the blessed one:[l] "Leave a blessing, my Lady Mary, to the world which thou art quitting, that those who make unto thee commemorations and offerings may be delivered from grievous afflictions."   Then my Lady Mary prayed and said: "May God, who willed of His own will and sent His Son, and He put on a body and dwelt in the palace of my members, have mercy upon the people[m] who call upon Him."   And again she prayed and said: "Our Lord Jesus, do Thou receive the prayers of the people who call upon Thee; and make bad times cease from the earth; and give a crown to old age, and bringing up to youth; and aid the souls that call upon Thee: and make bad times cease from the earth, when mankind, Lord, hold a commemoration to my body and spirit, which have quitted the earth; and make death and captivity and the sword and famine, and all calamities that befal mankind, pass away from the land in which offerings are offered to me; and make the pestilence cease from the land in which offerings are offered to me; and bless the garland of the year; and let these lands be preserved from locusts, that they may not devour them, and from blight and mildew and hailstones; and let every one who is sick, be healed; and who is afflicted, be relieved; and who is hungry, be satisfied; and whoever is captive through violence, let his bonds be loosed; and if any are sailing on the sea, and storms arise against them, and they call on the name of the Lord, let them be preserved from injury; and let those too who are in distant lands, and call upon my name, come (home) in safety.   Let the fields too, from which

---

[l] See Enger, p. 78, at the foot.   [m] *Lit.* "world."

offerings are offered in honour of me, be blessed and bring forth the seeds which are concealed in the furrows; and let the vines, from which wine is pressed in my name, bear good bunches (of grapes); and let there be concord and peace on all created beings that call on Thee. And let, O Lord, the garland of the years and the months be blessed before thee. And when the priests offer my offerings, receive their tithes with gladness; and make their churches thunder with thanksgiving, and let the Holy Spirit sing along with them. And on the kings be concord; and on the judges peace; and blessings and joys be on the face of the earth for ever and ever, Amen."

Then our Lord Jesus said to His mother: " Everything thou hast said to me, Mary, will I do to please thee; and 1 will show mercy to every one who calls upon thy name."

Then our Lord commanded Peter,[n] and he drew near to Him, and He said to him : " Now is the time; raise a psalm, and let all created beings sing with the voice of Halleluia." And when the created beings had sung with the voice of Halleluia, our Lord Jesus the Messiah prayed, and the holy angels gave glory. And straightway the soul of the blessed one departed from her, and He sent it to the mansions of the Father's house. And my Lady Mary said to her Son, as she was dying: " Fare Thee well, Rabbūlī! for lo, I am looking to Thy coming which is at hand." And Simon Cephas ran, and John the young, and Paul and Thomas; and straightway John laid his hands upon her eyes and closed them. And our Lord commanded them to place the blessed one in a chariot of light; and the twelve apostles bore it as it went to the Paradise of Eden.

And the apostles commanded[o] that there should be a commemoration of the blessed one three times in the year. On the twenty-fourth of the first Kānūn; "and because it is not possible that there should be a commemoration of her on the Nativity, we order that the commemoration of her shall take place two days after; and that with her pure offerings shall be blessed the seeds of the husbandmen, which they have borrowed and sown." And the disciples said that there should be a commemoration of the blessed one in the month of Iyār, on account of the seeds that were sown, and on account of the flying and creeping locusts, that they might not come forth and destroy the crops,[p] and so there be a famine and the people perish. And the Holy Spirit said to them: " They are[q] buried in the earth till the day appointed for them, which shall bring them forth, and

---

[n] See Enger, p. 82.   [o] Ibid., p. 100.   [p] *Lit.* " the world."
[q] *i. e.* the locusts, singular in Syriac.

they shall fulfil the will of their Lord. And when they are created, in a single hour shall they be created; and whithersoever they go to destroy, in one hour shall they desolate the earth." And the apostles ordered also that, on the Wednesday and Friday and Sunday of all the months of the year,[r] there should be prayers, and that these three days should be observed, and no work should be done on them. And the apostles ordered also that there should be a commemoration of the blessed one on the thirteenth of the month of Ab, [or on the fifteenth,] on account of the vines bearing bunches (of grapes), and on account of the trees bearing fruit, that clouds of hail, bearing stones of wrath, might not come, and the trees be broken, and their fruits, and the vines with their clusters. And the apostles also ordered[s] that any offering offered in the name of my Lady Mary should not remain over the night, but that at midnight of the night immediately preceding her commemoration, it should be kneaded and baked; and in the morning let it go up on the altar, whilst the people stand before the altar with psalms of David, and let the New and Old Testaments be read, and the volume of the decease of the blessed one; and let every one be before the altar in the church, and let the priests celebrate (the holy Eucharist)[t] and set forth the censer of incense and kindle the lights, and let the whole service be concerning these offerings; and when the whole service is finished, let every one take his offerings to his house. And let the priest speak thus : " In the name of the Father, and of the Son, and of the Holy Spirit, we celebrate the commemoration of my Lady Mary." Thus let the priest speak three times; and (simultaneously) with the word of the priest who speaks, the Holy Spirit shall come and bless these offerings; and when every one takes away his offering, and goes to his house, great help and the benison of the blessed one shall enter his dwelling and stablish it for ever.

And the apostles arose and set forth the censer of incense, and drew near to our Lord to beg of Him that the years with their months might be blessed. And they prayed, (saying :) "Our Lord Jesus the Messiah, hear the voice of our prayers, and bless the garland of the years and the months that are coming to the world, and bless the twelve months. Let *Nîsân* come, bearing the buds of good blossoms, that it may gladden the altars of the Lord with flowers. Let *Iyâr* come, bearing the spikes of ears (of corn) that are blessed, that of them there

---

[r] The meaning of this is not quite clear to me. Perhaps something may have been omitted.

[s] Compare Enger, p. 102.   [t] *Lit.* " offer."

may be an offering to the Lord. Let *Hazīrān* come, bearing tables of rubbed out (ears),ᵘ and carrying dishes full of new bread. Let *Tāmūz* come, giving thanks because of men, who are singing in the threshing-floors, which are full of thanks-givings and rejoicings. Let *Ab* come, giving worship to God, who has blessed and given it unripe and ripe (fruits). Let *Ilūl* come, worshipping and praising the Messiah, who has blessed the months and the years. Let (the first) *Teshrīn* come, praising and glorifying Him who has heard the voice of the husbandman, who has sown with the ploughᵛ of the cross. Let (the second) *Teshrīn* come, and its good things with it, which cometh rejoicing from heaven, fattening and blessing the earth and its inhabitants. Let (the first) *Kānūn* come, and its good things with it, thick clouds, and lightnings, and rain, which is diffused over the face of the earth. Let (the second) *Kānūn* come, and with it snow and ice, which gladdens the earth. Let *Shĕbāt* come, bearing on its shoulders good things that give birth to joys. Let *Adār* come, carrying presents to the Lord, choice lambs and sheep, giving thanks."

Thus prayed the apostles and said: "Yea, Lord God, who didst send Thy son to the world to restore it to life out of error, let Thy blessing be upon the earth and its inhabitants; and let Thy grace come unto us and manifest itself to us at this time." Then our Lord Jesus came unto them and said to them:ʷ "Fear not, ye blessed; everything that ye ask shall be given to you, and at all times your wish shall be with your Father who is in heaven." Then the apostles bowed their heads and asked a blessing from our Lord Jesus.

And the apostles rose from the place in which they were praying, and said: "Come, let us go down from the Mount of

---

ᵘ See Lev. ii. 14, 16 ; xxiii. 14 ; Ruth ii. 14.

ᵛ ܨܡܕܐ or ܨܡܕܬܐ, ἄροτρον, *e.g.* in the *Gospel of Thomas*, cap. xiii., καὶ ἐποίει ἐν τῷ καιρῷ ἐκείνῳ ἄροτρα καὶ ζυγούς, Syr. ܐܢܕܝܡܐ ܡܟܪܬ ܠܐ. ܚܙܡ ܗܘܐ. ܐܠܐ ܨܡܕܐ ܘܢܝܪܐ. So also Mār Jacob of Serūg in his discourse on the city of Antioch (Add. 14,590, fol. 34 *a*, ܨܡܐ ܠܘܨܐ ܢܪܨ ܐܢܬ ܕܣܘܪܝܘܣܐ ܨܡܨܚܐ; and again fol. 36 *b*, ܠܘܥܛܐ ܪܟܡܛܐ ܨܡܨܐ . ܚܩܡܐ ܘܡܟܠܚܐ ܚܣܐ ܕܣܘܡܚܐ ܕܣܡܨܛܐ. ܢܥܡ ܐܢܟܐ ܐܩܕܐ ܕܣܘܨܟܡܐܬܐ. Add. 7203, النِير الخَشَبَة التي فوق فوق ܨܡܨܐ. القَدَان المِشان (sic) ويسمَّي بالعربِّية القيقن وهي آلة الفَلَاح.

ʷ Compare Enger, p. 102.

Olives to the cave at the head of the valley, and let us write there how my Lady Mary was crowned in the cloud of light." And the apostles went down from the Mount of Olives to the cave at the head of the valley, and set forth incense, and commanded that a book should be written as follows: " We all of us, the apostles, testify before God, and before our Lord Jesus the Messiah, and before the Holy Spirit, that our Lord Jesus the Messiah did these miracles before His mother, when she was departing from the world." And there were written concerning her six books, each book by two of the apostles, all the signs and all the miracles which my Lady Mary did. This book was written in Hebrew and Greek and Latin; and the apostles deposited it with Mār John, whose blessing is great.

And the apostles prayed and called on our Lord Jesus to come and bless them,* that each of them might go to the country whence he had come. And they prayed a long while, and our Lord came to them, and blessed them, and ascended to heaven.

And the twelve apostles asked of Paul and of Peter, and said: "Because we apostles are twelve, it is fitting that twelve copies should be written of this book of my Lady Mary, and that a copy should go along with each of us." Peter said to the apostles his fellows: "These others of us who are dead,—who, behold, are going to their graves,—shall we write for them the book of my Lady Mary?" The apostles said to Peter: "What dost thou order us to do?" Peter said: "Let each of us, when he has gone to the place whence he came, write and teach the people, to whom he has gone, whatever the Holy Spirit puts into his mouth; and let him teach these things, that there may be a commemoration of my Lady Mary three times in the year."

And John, whose blessing is great, took the book of the departure of the blessed one. And Paul and Peter called, and spoke to John between themselves; the apostles Paul, Peter and John spoke to one another, wishing to divide the volume. And as they were going to have a dispute about it, a voice came to them from heaven, which said: "Go in peace, ye blessed, to the places whence ye came, and your Lord will do your pleasure, whatever it be that ye want." Then there appeared to them lightnings and thunderings from heaven, singing before the disciples and going to the places whence they came. And those too who were dead and had arisen, went back to their graves; and the blessed ones slept and were at rest.

Through the prayer of the prophets and apostles, martyrs and confessors, may every one who believes in the Father and in

---

* Compare Enger, p. 86.

the Son and in the Holy Spirit, and in my Lady Mary, the mother of God, and in the Church, the bride of the Messiah, and in the convents, the dwellings of the just, receive a blessing from our Lord Jesus the Messiah, who was born of Mary the Virgin. And may every one, who commemorates her, be remembered in heaven. And may our Lord Jesus the Messiah show mercy and compassion upon all our congregation, which has heard these holy words, for ever and ever, Amen. Here ends the fourth book.

BOOK FIFTH.

When the blessed one was placed in the Paradise of Eden[v] and was crowned with this great glory, and the apostles had departed in all directions, our Lord Jesus came to his mother into the Paradise of Eden. And the chariots of the angels descended from heaven in infinite numbers, and the Paradise of Eden was covered, and all the mountains that were around it. And the sound of nothing was heard save the voice of those saying, Holy! holy! holy! And when our Lord came to my Lady Mary, he called to her and said: "Mary, rise." And straightway she was restored to life and worshipped Him. And our Lord Jesus said to her: "To show thee the glory of my Father's house I am come to thee." The blessed Mary said to Him: "'Tis well, Rabbūlī." And Elias the prophet came to our Lord and to my Lady Mary, and Enoch and Moses and Simon Cephas: these came at the beck of our Saviour to the Paradise of Eden. And our Lord said to His mother: "Mary, examine and see what I have prepared for the just who love me." And the blessed one saw the mansions of the just, how they were built and decorated and beautified; and she saw the banquet-halls of the martyrs; and she looked on the glorious mansion in which the righteous abode; and she saw the lovely trees of Paradise, how beautiful they were in appearance and how pleasant was the smell of their branches; and how perfumes were diffused from tree to tree, and a sweet fragrance was wafted from branch to branch. And our Lord Jesus plucked some of the delicious fruit of these trees and gave it to her, that she might taste of these fruits that were reared by the Holy Spirit.

These things my Lady Mary saw in the Paradise of Eden. And straightway the cherub of the sword cried out and spake; and our Lord said to His mother: "Come, ascend and see the heaven in which is the glory of my Father; and thou shalt

---

. [v] See Enger, p. 88.

enter and see the heaven of heavens and the waters which are above the heaven; and thou shalt ascend on above the waters, and see the decorated Jerusalem, the palace of my Father in which He dwells." And our Lord Jesus the Messiah was sitting in a chariot of light, he and my Lady Mary his mother; and one cloud carried Elias the prophet, and another Enoch, and another Simon Cephas, and another John the young; and they ascended on wheels of fire that overpowered the sun, and entered this lowest heaven. And my Lady Mary saw there that all the store-houses of God were there; the house of ice and snow and frost; the house of rain and dew and heat; the house of winds and lightnings and blasts; the house of clouds and whirlwinds, the servants of God that proclaim his commands. And she saw the place in which Elias the prophet used to dwell and pray. These things my Lady Mary saw in this lower heaven.

And she ascended and saw the heaven of heavens and the waters above the heavens. And on above the waters she ascended, and saw Jerusalem that is in heaven,* which has twelve walls and twelve gates, named after the twelve apostles; and at each door stands an apostle, with angels and archangels, who are standing and glorifying. And at the outer gate of Jerusalem there are spiritual beings without number, glorifying with their trumpets, along with Abraham, Isaac, and Jacob, and Mār David the singer. And they drew near and worshipped before the king the Messiah and before His mother, as she entered and saw the heavenly Jerusalem. She entered the *first* gate, and was worshipped by the angels. And she entered the *second* gate, and the prayer of the cherubim was offered to her. She entered the *third* gate, and the prayer of the seraphim was offered to her. She entered the *fourth* gate, and was worshipped by the family of the archangels. She entered the *fifth* gate, and the lightnings and thunders uttered praises before her. She entered the *sixth* gate, and they cried before her, Holy, holy, holy! She entered the *seventh* gate, and fire and flame worshipped before her. And she entered the *eighth* gate, and the rain and dew worshipped her. And she entered the *ninth* gate, and Gabriel and Michael worshipped her. And she entered the *tenth* gate, and the sun and moon worshipped her. And she entered the *eleventh* gate, and all the apostles worshipped and praised her. And she entered the *twelfth* gate, and the Son, who was born of her, strengthened her and blessed her.

---

* See Enger, p. 90.

Thus my Lady Mary entered the heavenly Jerusalem, and worshipped before God the Father. In that hour my Lady Mary saw the Holy Father and the beloved Son and the Holy Spirit the Paraclete, the Father being glorified by His Son and the Son by the Father, and the Holy Spirit between the two of them.

Then our Lord Jesus the Messiah drew near and took His mother and showed her hidden and terrible things; and showed her what eye hath not seen nor ear heard, and what hath not entered into the heart of man, what God hath prepared for them that love Him at the day of the resurrection.[a] And He showed her glories that proclaim concerning miracles, and miracles that cry out concerning glories; and hidden things that cry out concerning revealed things, and revealed things that cry out concerning hidden things. And He took her and entered within the extreme limit of all created things;[b] and He showed her and said: "Here is the place where Enoch dwells, and to here have I removed him, and this is the place in which he prays." Here ends the fifth book.

Book Sixth.

And the blessed one lifted up her eyes[c] and saw the two worlds, this one that passeth away, and that one which passeth not away. And she saw too, in a place in that world which passeth not away, many lights shining very brightly, and mansions without number; and between one mansion and another a great scent of perfumes was diffused, and there were trumpets sounding over the mansions. And she saw the tabernacles of the just, and multitudes standing on this side of these tabernacles. My Lady Mary said to the Messiah, "My Lord Rabbūlī, what are these?" The Messiah said to my Lady Mary: "These are the tabernacles of the just, and these lights are shining in their honour; and from a distance they behold their happiness, until the day of the resurrection, when they shall inherit their mansions."

And again my Lady Mary saw another place which was very dark, and an exceeding great smoke was going up from it, and a smell of sulphur was diffused around it, and a strong fire was blazing in it. And the sound of that fire was going like heavy

-----

[a] Compare 1 Cor. ii. 9.

[b] See Enger, p. 92, line 16, where for مُقيم read مُقَيّب.

[c] See Enger, p. 92.

thunder, when it is overhead in the heavens and is listened to with terror; so was coming the sound of that fire, which was kindled for the wicked. And men were standing on this side of that darkness, and weeping and in sorrow, as they stood at a distance. My Lady Mary said to the Messiah: "My Lord Rabbūlī, what are these?" The Messiah said to the blessed one: "This that is roaring is Gehenna, which is kindled for the wicked; and these who are standing and looking upon it are the sinners; and from a distance they are beholding their torment, and knowing for what they are reserved at the last day; for the day of judgment is not yet come, that they should receive the inheritance of darkness; and at the time of the judgment, those who have neglected my commands, which I commanded them, and have not listened to me, shall be tormented in this Gehenna." And as my Lady Mary was standing, and our Lord Jesus beside her, she heard the voice of the just, who were saying: "Glory to Thee, Thou good God, who givest a recompence to the just, who call on Thy name, at the day of judgment." And the wicked also cried out beside that darkness, by which they were standing, and said: "Have mercy on us, Son of God, righteous judge, when Thou comest to dissolve heaven and earth." Then, when my Lady Mary heard the voice of the just, she was glad; and when she heard the voice of the wicked, she was very sorry. And she besought the Messiah, and offered up a prayer for the sinners, and said: "Rabbūlī, have mercy upon the wicked when Thou judgest them at the day of judgment; for I have heard their voice and am grieved."

And our Lord Jesus took his mother,[d] and came to the Paradise of Eden, with multitudes of the supernals. And my Lady Mary called Mār John the young, and told him everything that our Lord Jesus had shown to her; and she said to John: "Guard these things which thy Lord hath shown me; for at the time when they are to be revealed and I tell thee, these words shall go forth, and the books of my glorious deeds, that there may be to me commemorations and offerings among men. Because, at times when afflictions abound among men, and there are famines and wars, and the earth quakes for the sins of wicked men, who are destroying it by nefarious deeds; at that time, abounding in affliction to mankind, the air of heaven shall be dark, and winds and whirlwinds shall blow; and the sun shall be dark at mid-day; and the times shall be hateful; and in the nights visions shall be seen; and there shall be a destruction of mankind by one another; and bitter plagues shall be sent upon

---

[d] See Enger, p. 96, line 1—3, and p. 102, line 17.

creation; and the Son the Messiah shall come to the world, and shall not find belief prevailing in the mouth of men."

These things, and more than these, did our Lord Jesus the Messiah reveal to my Lady Mary; and my Lady Mary revealed them to Mār John the young. And our Lord Jesus said to my Lady Mary his mother: "Blessed art thou, Mary, because of what thine eyes have seen, and what thou art about to see; because afflictions shall abound unto men, and those who call on thy name shall be delivered from destruction." And my Lady Mary said to the Messiah: "True are thy words, Rabbūlī, because they are from the holy mouth of Thy Father; and everything that Thou didst say to me, when Thou wast upon earth, is true and fulfilled; and every one who believes on Thee shall with Thee inherit the glory that is for ever, which the children of light inherit and the just look for, who praise Thee and Thy Father and Thy Holy Spirit in heaven and in earth." Here ends the sixth book. There are finished in this volume the six books of the Departure of my Lady Mary from the world. Glory be to the Father, and to the Son, and to the Holy Spirit, for ever and ever, Amen.

———

⁂ The reader is requested to correct the three following misprints in the Syriac text. Page ܒ, line 12, read ܠܐܤܐ instead of ܠܐܤ. Page ܠܐ, line 8, read ܩܕܐܡܝܐ. Page ܣܝ, line 12, read ܢܬܠܩܘܢ.

www.ingramcontent.com/pod-product-compliance
Lightning Source LLC
Chambersburg PA
CBHW030901260626
47169CB00008B/2628